**Ernest Quare with his harriers, wife, daughter and groom,
Matching Green, c.1898**

A Quinton

ii

An Account of Daniel Quare, 1648-1724

Clockmaker of Exchange Alley, London, and his Descendants from 1734 to 1903, who were Farmers of Matching, Essex.

Patrick Streeter

The Matching Press

in association with the Lavers and District Local History Society

Harlow

2020

Published by
The Matching Press
in association with the Lavers and District Local History Society

Watermans End Cottage
Matching Green, Harlow
Essex CM17 0RQ
UK

Tel 01279 731308
Email: Sptstreeter@aol.com

Illustration on cover:
Matching Green from The Illustrated Sporting and Dramatic News, April 1885.
Tudor Quare's maltings can be seen on the far right.
Illustrations on back cover: The Essex Hunt by Daniel Wolstenholme.

Printed in Great Britain by
Simmonds Printers, 9 Bilton Road, Chelmsford, Essex, CM1 2UJ.

British Library Cataloguing in Publication Data 978-0-9518664-8-1
Streeter, Patrick

Contents

Acknowledgements

I would like to thank the many people who helped me with this publication. In particular Tudor Quare, Bruce Quare, Andy and Fiona Barnard, Cedric Martin, Terry Page of Forge Cottage, Matching, Michael Wood of the Essex Yeomanry Association, Sir George White, Guy Boney QC, Penny Graves, Anna Rolls of the Clockmaker's Company, Wendy Hibbett of Writtle Archives, Martin Figg of MFP Marketing, Michael and Christine Collins, Peter Wheeler, Andrew Tatham, and Ray Jensen of Victoria, Australia.

Patrick Streeter
Matching Green
October 2020

aniel Quare, 1648-1724, was one of this country's finest clockmakers and worked during a golden age of clockmaking. His work is to be found in royal collections and leading museums, and commands impressive prices at auction. He was born in 1648 to a Quaker family, and at the age of 23 was admitted as a member of the Clockmakers' Company in London. His birthplace was reputedly Somerset. There is no proof of this but if you search on the genealogical websites in the sixteenth century, you come up with two clusters of Quares, one in Yorkshire and another in the Somerset villages of Croscombe and Misterton. There are no Daniels there, but Somerset is a likely birthplace. The name Quare is rare and may have the same origin as the name Quarry; that is, a person who lives near or works in a quarry. Five years later he married Mary, daughter of Jeremiah Stevens, a maltster of High Wycombe, and he lived and worked at St. Martin's-le-Grand, a short walk from St. Paul's. His Quaker faith led him into conflict with the authorities. In 1678 he refused to pay a rate for the maintenance of the clergy and was fined £2.12s.6d, which he also refused to pay and so he had goods valued at £6 seized. The next year he was fined again for refusing to contribute to the cost of the militia, and two clocks and two watches were taken from him. In 1680 he invented the repeating watch movement, and two years later he moved to Lombard Street, and then finally to Exchange Alley where many watchmakers had their premises.

In 1683 he was in trouble with the authorities again. Together with five other Quakers he had goods to the value of £195.17s.6d seized for attending a meeting at White Hart Court. In spite of his dissident behaviour he found favour with William III, for whom he made a longcase clock for his bedroom at Hampton Court Palace, where it still stands.

**A drawing of William III's Bedroom in Hampton Court Palace in 1885
showing Daniel's clock in the far corner**

Being a bedroom clock it does not strike but it will go for a year without rewinding, and it shows sundial time and latitude and longitude together with the course of the sun. In 1695 he invented and patented the portable barometer. It could be carried anywhere and turned upside down without disturbing the mercury. There are another two barometers of his at Hampton Court; a conventional one and an angled one with a thermometer. Between February 1716 and the latter part of 1717 Daniel, with the support of the Clockmakers' Company, was involved in litigation with Charles Clay of Stockton, Yorkshire. Charles had petitioned parliament for a patent on a repeating musical watch. This was successfully opposed by Daniel on the grounds that an invention of his was first. Daniel was offered the Royal Warrant but declined because, as a practising Quaker,

2

he could not take the Oath of Allegiance, but he was made 'free of the backstairs' at the Royal Palaces which meant he had easy access to carry out his duties.

In 1697 he became an Assistant at the Clockmakers' Company; in 1705 a Warden and, three years later, Master. In 1709 he took on Stephen Horseman as an apprentice and in 1718 introduced him as a partner. Another Daniel Quare[2] was also apprenticed to him, who was not his son. (Many members of the family have been given the same Christian names. The small number will differentiate one from another) This Daniel never graduated to be a member of the Company. He could have been a nephew, and crops up together with his father, Robert, and mother, Mary, in the list of inhabitants of London in 1695. Daniel had one surviving son, Jeremiah, and three surviving daughters: Elizabeth, Sarah and Anna. Elizabeth married Silvanus Bevan in 1715. Silvanus was a successful apothecary and founded the pharmaceutical firm of Allen and Hanbury. Their wedding was a very splendid affair, which is surprising for Quakers. It took place at the Quaker Meeting House in Gracechurch Street and over one hundred people signed the wedding certificate including the Ambassadors of Sicily and Venice, Sarah, Duchess of Marlborough, Lord Finch and a sprinkling of foreign nobles. Another signatory was Mr John Peckethman, who was to lose his Daniel Quare tortoiseshell watch with a greyhound crest in Mile End five years later. It was a Quaker custom for all the guests to sign the marriage certificate, and at the end of the signatures is written, 'and a large party from the Court'. After the marriage the guests dined at Skinners Hall where the bride and groom made accomplished speeches. Elizabeth died in childbirth the next near. One reason Daniel was able to afford such a sumptuous wedding is given by Walter Thornbury in his book, *Old and New London*. He suggests that Daniel, as a side line, made a lot of money speculating on the Stock Exchange. He was certainly in a good position to pick up tips as his shop was only a few hundred feet from the exchange. Silvanus married again but never had any more children. Daniel had a country house at Croydon where he died at the age of 76. Stephen carried on his business but he was a better craftsman than businessman and went bankrupt in 1733. The business was taken over by Richard Peckover who traded from the Royal Exchange until 1754. It is likely that the premises shown in the attached map as Richard Peckover's was that occupied by Daniel, especially as he is described sometimes as 'by the King's Arms', and the King's Arms was in Exchange Alley.

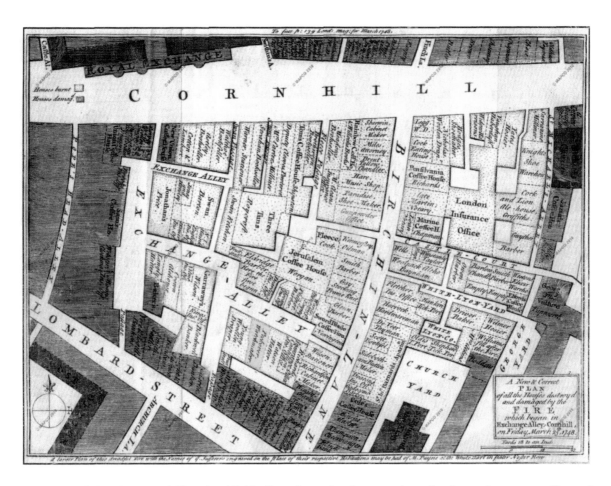

A map of Exchange Alley in 1748 showing the layout just before the great fire of that year. Richard Peckover's shop is shown in yellow and this is probably the site occupied by Daniel Quare.

It was thought that no portrait of Daniel existed, but in November 2014 at Bonham's auction rooms, twenty five ivory models by Silvanus Bevan, Daniel's son-in-law, came up on the market. Silvanus was not only a successful apothecary but a talented carver. The portraits include such luminaries as Sir Hans Sloane, Sir Isaac Newton, William Penn, the Duchess of Marlborough and Daniel.

**Twenty five Ivory Reliefs by Silvanus Bevan.
Daniel is on the second row in the centre.**

Daniel's Ivory Portrait

The Georgians were rather careless about their personal property. Between 1703 and 1760 there were eleven advertisements in the London papers reporting lost or stolen Daniel Quare watches; eight had been lost and three were stolen. Here are a few examples:

From *The Post Man and the Historical Account*, 9.2.1703

"Yesterday there was dropt a pendulum silver watch, in a silver box without a case, the name D.Quare, London on the outer plate. On the middle plate, Quare, London; number upon the watch and inside of the box, 2490. If the party that took it up will bring it to Daniel Quare, watchmaker in Exchange Alley, London, he or she shall receive a 20s reward."

From *The Post Boy*, 11.3.1714

"Whereas on Sunday the 28th of last month in the morning a GOLD WATCH made by Daniel Quare, No. 2538, with a cypher K.W. engraved upon the gold outer case was taken from a gentlewoman's side at or coming out of St. Edmund the King, Lombard Street. If anyone will bring the said watch to Daniel Quare, watchmaker in Exchange Alley, London they shall have ten pound reward, and no questions asked, or if bought already then their money again with refundable profit."

From *The Daily Courant*, 23.12.1718.

"Lost or dropt from a gentlewoman's side on Thursday the 18th instant, going out of a coach at Ludgate Hill or in Essex Street a gold watch made by Daniel Quare, and M.R. on the inside case in a cypher, with a Spanish gold chain, a locket and a Bath metal seal, with two Coats of Arms on a lozenge on it. If offered to be sold or valued pray stop them and give notice to Mr Brand, Goldsmith, in Lombard Street, and you have 4 guineas reward, and no questions asked."

From *The Daily Courant*, 7.5.1712

"Charles Guill, a Guernsey man, speaks French well, aged about 35 or 40 years, a tall, lean, raw-boned, broad-shouldered man of pale lean visage, and thin-jaw'd of a frowning, down-looked countenance, inclined to a stooping in his walk, somewhat hesitating in his speech, wearing a grey cloth suit with silver-fronted buttons, or a cinnamon-coloured suit and a light tyed up wig, formerly used the sea, since lived with Mr Snell, the writing-master, and since that, for these two years has belonged to the Bank of England, from whose service he withdrew himself on Saturday last on the 3rd instant, with several Exchequer Bills and bank notes. He is supposed to have about him a new gold repeating watch made by Daniel Quare, numbered 426, in a gold case. Whoever shall apprehend him, for as he may be secured, shall thereupon receive from Mr Thomas Medocks, Cashier of the Bank of England the sum of £100, or, if he will return, he will be favourably received."

The hapless Mr Guill was apprehended near Stony Stratford ten days later.

From *The Daily Courant*, 20.1.1720

"Lost at Mile End on Sunday the 10th instant between 5 and 6 in the evening, a silver watch made by Daniel Quare, No 4832, and a tortoiseshell watch and a triangle seal, the arms and crest being the two Greyhound heads, and a gold plain ring. Whoever will bring or send the abovementioned to Mr John Pinkethman's in Exchange Alley, shall have eight guineas for the whole, or two guineas for the ring, and no questions asked."

From *The Daily Advertiser*, 21.11.1743

"Whereas a gold repeating watch was taken from a gentleman last Saturday near the Friary, St. James's made by Daniel Quare, with a seal to it with three cinquefoils, the crest an Antelope's head; whoever may bring it to Major General Hamilton, at his house near Burlington Gardens, shall receive 8 guineas reward, and no questions asked."

Another of Daniel's watches, No 838, was lost near his shop in December 1720. All his watches were numbered so one can work out the date when they were made. It may be that some of these lost or stolen watches, identifiable by their number, are to be found in collections today, and this little bit of their history will add to their interest.

Daniel's pieces often attracted incompetent thieves. A contemporary incident occurred in July 2009. A thief unscrewed a 1695 ivory Quare barometer from the wall of the Fairfax museum in York, left a few fingerprints, then put it under his overcoat in full view of the CCTV. He was arrested a few days later and sentenced to two years.

YEfterday there was dropt a Pendulum Silver minute Watch, in a Silver Box wffhout a Cafe, the
Name D. Quare, London, on the upper Plate, on the middle, Plate Quare London; number upon the Watch and infide
of the Box 2490. If the Party that took it up, will bring it
to Daniel Quare, Watchmaker, in Exchange-alley, London;
he or fhe fhall receive 20 s. reward.

An Example of a lost clock advertisement

In 1744, a Quare and Horseman watch, No 569, had quite an adventure. Before highwaymen and other felons were taken to Tyburn to be hung, they were encouraged to make a written confession which was then published. Robert Rochead was one of these. He entered our story as follows. He was born of a good family in Edinburgh and as a young man went to sea, but a liking for wild living led him into an extraordinary career as a highwayman and pirate in England, Virginia and the West Indies. In 1744 he was back in England living with a lady of doubtful virtue, Sarah Lowther. Money was short so he, with an accomplice, on a Sunday morning, hired two horses and took the Chatham Road intending to rob some Navy clerks of sailors' wages or perhaps the takings from landlords, received from the Navy recently in port. But the fleet was late in coming in and they turned home for London. On their way they met a coach at Blackheath and held it up, taking the Quare watch, a gold ring and £8. They made for *The Blue Maid* in the Borough where they gave a shilling to a groom to take the horses back to Smithfield. Robert's downfall came when he heard that one of his accomplices decided to give Queen's evidence against him. Together with a fellow villain, Walter Nagle, he fled to Cowes, the Isle of Wight, and enlisted on a ship, but was arrested there and put in irons on a man of war, *HMS Shrewsbury*. He lay there for six weeks and then was taken, handcuffed, in a coach to Newgate. He was tried, found guilty and sentenced to death, but, thanks to clemency from the King, the sentence was changed to transportation for 14 years.

Some Examples of Daniel's Clocks and Barometers

An Early 18th Century Quarter-repeating Table Clock, No.218

A Silver pair case verge Alarm Watch, No 272, first quarter 18th century

Walnut Veneered Table Clock, 1690

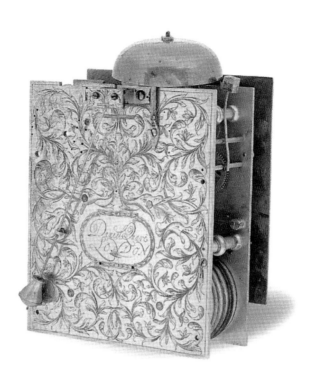

Rear View of Walnut Table Clock

A c.1718 Miniature Travelling Wall Alarm Timepiece,
Quare and Horseman, No.178

A Quare Barometer, c.1700, from the Science Museum Collection

An 18th Century Japanned Longcase Clock, decorated with Gold Chinnoiseries, No.154, from the collection of the Spanish Manso de Velasco family, Counts of Superunda

Details of the Coat of Arms on the Manso de Velasco Clock

A Gold-Cased Pocket Watch, No.2913, c.1705

The Watch Closed

**Longcase Clock with Oak Case, Veneered with Burr Walnut, c.1700.
Made for William III, Royal Collection, Hampton Court**

Daniel's son, Jeremiah, was born in 1683. He did not become a craftsman like his father but a merchant, trading in the East Indies, Virginia and Barbados. He was a member of the Glover's Company but that did not necessarily mean that he traded as a glover, as citizens would join a Livery Company and obtain the Freedom of the City of London so that they could do business within the City walls. He married Ann Braine, daughter of Benjamin Braine, who bought the Stock Hall estate, a manor in the parish of Matching, Essex, in 1710. This was a propitious marriage as the Braines were a leading Essex family. James, Anne's brother, was High Sheriff of Essex in 1724. Jeremiah had one surviving son, Daniel, whom we shall call Daniel[3], who was born in 1708 and who married Elizabeth Braine, daughter of James. She was an heiress who inherited Stock Hall. A Poll Book has Daniel[3] owning land in Matching in 1734. We know quite a lot about the estate as a fine map of it was made in 1753 by James Dodson, and there is a schedule of its holdings in the Essex Record Office. A copy of the map is owned by a Matching family. Matching Green is triangular and Daniel[3] owned all the houses on the north and west sides.

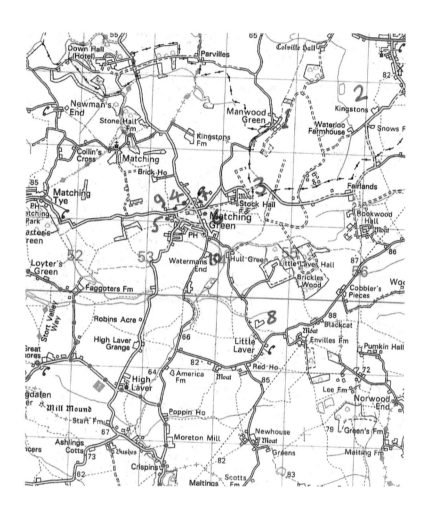

Map of Matching Green.
The houses occupied by the Quares were
(1) Manwood Green Farm,
(2) Kingstons Farm,
(3) Stock Hall,
(4) Honington House,
(5) Hazeldene, later Lascelles Lodge,
(6) The Limes and (7) Maytrees,
(8) Little Laver Hall Farm,
(9) 'The Cottage', now Wingates.
(10) Watermans End.
Daniel[3] owned all the houses on the north and west side of the Green.

Stock Hall.
There were originally two wings. The east has now been restored.

Daniel's[3] tenants were:

Dennis Butcher – 2 acres
Mr Chalk – 15 acres
John Little, Blacksmith
Widow Biggs
Thomas Smith
Widow Petts
Bolted the wheeler
John Shires

James Boreham – 9 acres
Joseph Boultwood, Clockmaker
Thomas Biggs
John Cheshire
Cornelius Hoyle
James Hasty – a garden
John Clark

James Hasty was a shopkeeper. The most interesting of these tenants is Joseph Boultwood, the clockmaker. It was unusual, but not unheard of, for a clockmaker to trade from a village rather than a town, where he would be nearer to his suppliers and customers. A good example of one of Joseph's clocks now belongs to the current owners of Stock Hall. His clocks are rare but the *Essex Journal* in 1967 reported that there were examples in Buckhurst Hill and Warley.

Joseph Boultwood's Longcase Clock, showing his signature

Joseph Boultwood's Longcase Clock

**The Ordnance Survey map of Matching Green in 1875
showing where Daniel[3] Quare's tenants lived in 1753**

In the *London Gazette* of 1737 there is a report of a bankruptcy of a Daniel Quare, Merchant, of Goldman's Fields, London. This could be the Daniel[3] who married Elizabeth Braine and whose fortune then transformed him from a man of straw to a man of property, or it could be a descendant of the Daniel Quare who was apprenticed to the clockmaker Daniel[1] in 1707, or indeed that Daniel himself. Anyway, the *Gazette* of 1740 records that a farm called Hotts or Hoates Farm (now called Holts Farm) of 140 acres in Little Horkesly, five miles from Colchester, is to be sold for the benefit of the creditors. However, the Quare family managed to hold on to it as it was sold by one of them to George Sadler in 1772. Daniel[3] sold Stock Hall to William Selwin, an ancestor of Lord

Rookwood, in 1755. Kingstons Farm in Matching may have come with Elizabeth Brain's dowry as well, as Daniel[3] and his son Benjamin[2] sold this to Selwin in 1754 for £4,400. It is not clear why the Quares were selling land at this time. They continued to farm much of it as tenants. Maybe William Selwin was so flush with money that he had made in the City that he was prepared to pay a price well over the odds.

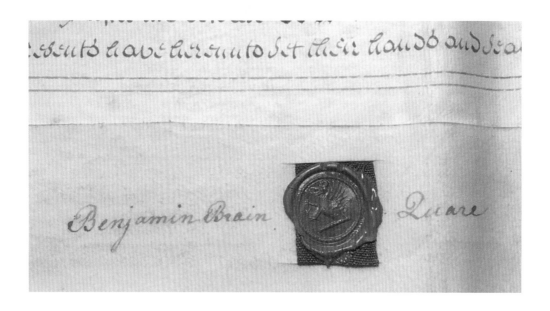

**Daniel[3] and Benjamin[2]'s Signatures on the Sale Deed
when Kingstons Farm was sold to William Selwin in 1754,
together with the Quare crest of a Griffin with a spear on a seal**

William Selwin was a silk merchant of Paternoster Row in London. He was involved in City politics and became Receiver of Land Taxes for the City and the County of Middlesex in 1734.[1] In Georgian England, collecting taxes could be a remunerative occupation. He bought the Down Hall estate for £4,500 in 1741 and the Selwin estate was to dominate the parishes of Matching and Hatfield Broad Oak. In the 1870s, at its height, together with the Ibbotson properties, it stretched to 2,098 acres in Essex and Yorkshire. It was sold by William's descendant, Captain Calverley, in a series of sales in the 1920s and 1930s.

In the late 1700s and early 1800s we see a number of the members of the Quare family establishing themselves in Matching. In 1836 the *Tithe Commutation Act* was passed, and details of tithe awards together with detailed maps were drawn up for every parish. The table below shows the awards for members of the Quare family. Tudor Brain Quare does not feature. This is probably because he did not acquire his holdings until after the awards were made. The entries for Daniel Quare cover father and son as their stewardship overlapped the period of the awards.

Tithe Awards c. 1845   Return of Owners of Land 1872

	Henry Tudor Hewitt Quare	Henry Quare	Daniel Quare, father & son	Tudor Quare	Total
Hatfield Broad Oak	95.2.3				95.2.3
White Roding		75.1.35			75.1.35
High Laver			2.3.29		2.3.29
Little Laver		2.3.4			2.3.4
Matching		176.0.35			176.0.35
Willingale Doe			34.2.29		34.2.29
Total	95.2.3	254.1.34	37.2.18		387.2.15
Acreage	174.1.6	171.0.1	19.3.36	42.1.19	407.2.22
Rental Value £.s.d	**337.10**	**138.19**	**28.6**	**44.5**	**£549.00**

The measurements are in acres, roods and perches. There are 40 perches to a rood and 4 roods to an acre. Benjamin[4] Quare, 1789-1855, was a tenant of Henry Quare at Maytrees occupying one rood and three perches.

Schedule of Tithe Awards made between 1837 and 1850

---

[1]William died in 1768 aged 82. There is a fine marble memorial to him in Hatfield Broad Oak church. He outlived four sons and a daughter, just leaving one daughter, Jane. The epitaph reads, *'He was a Merchant in the City of London to which profession he did immortal honour by his unceasing vigilance and his unerring probity.'* In view of the fortune he made from tax collecting one may want to take this epitaph with a pinch of salt.

Daniel[3] had three surviving sons: Daniel[4], Benjamin Braine[2] and Jeremiah. This Daniel[4], although resident in Matching, owned farms in Willingale Doe and Willingale Spain. These two are interesting villages in that their two churches are adjacent to each other and share the same churchyard. This occurred because the D'Espania family of Spains Hall built the first one in the 12th century. In the 14th century the D'Ou family came to live in Willingale. At that time the wool industry was flourishing in Essex, and the village population had greatly increased. The old church was too small and, rather than pull it down, a new one was built nearby. Daniel[4]'s farms were Bowyers, Blunts and Marshalls, and the manor of Warden's Hall, together with fields called Elliots and Mashbury Shots. Another beneficiary was his nephew, Benjamin Braine[2]. When he died, although he lived in Matching, Daniel[3] was buried in Willingale.

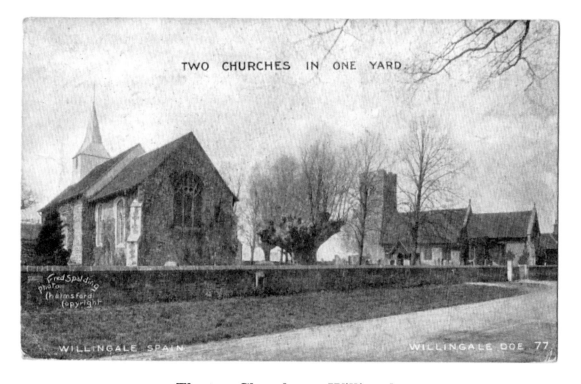

The two Churches at Willingale

Daniel[3]'s second son, Benjamin Braine[2] was born in Stepney in 1731. (It is hoped the reader is not too confused by the proliferation of Daniels and Benjamins. Please refer to the family trees for elucidation). He was described as a merchant of Tottenham High Cross. In 1753, with his father, he petitioned parliament for permission to sell the families' interest in East New Jersey in North America. This gives some indication of what sort of business the Quares were in at this time. He married Ann Petts[2] of Hatfield Broad Oak and settled in Matching, where he died in 1774. Daniel[3] had one other surviving son, Jeremiah, who was born in Whitechapel in 1732 and lived until 1765. In Daniel[4]'s will of 1831, we find out about his three sons: Daniel[5] of Houndsditch who was a carver and guilder; David of Oxford Street, a coach builder; and Edward, also a coachmaker. Edward had four children, whose names all began with E, which may have caused some confusion: another Edward, Eliza, Emma and Emily. Daniel[5] was in partnership with his father as a carver and guilder and took over the business in 1817. He had one surviving son, another Daniel[6] who lived from 1784 to 1848. Benjamin Braine[2] had a son, another Benjamin Braine[3], 1766-1856, a surgeon who married Marianne Hewitt. The Quares were now firmly establishing themselves as farmers and minor gentry in the Matching area and they became great followers of foxhunting, and were proficient cricketers. Recorded in the *Essex Standard* of 20 and 27 July 1833 are reports of two matches when Matching played against West Essex and four Quares played: Henry, Tudor[1], Daniel[6] and Alfred, and also a Raincock, from a family of Stockbrokers, who was related to them by marriage. At the first fixture at Navestock all the first innings' wickets went to a Quare; nine for Henry and one for Tudor. At the return match at Matching on the following Saturday, Alfred got four wickets, Henry two and Daniel[6] one. Later on, Tudor[1]'s grandson, also Tudor[2], was to form his own team which played at Matching.

Their hunting exploits are chronicled in two books, *The Essex Foxhounds* by Tresham Gilbey and Richard Ball, published in 1896, and *Leaves from a Hunting Diary* by Harry Beauchamp Yerburgh published in 1900. Henry Quare lived to be 85 and hunted up until ten days before his death. When he died, the venue of the opening meet was changed from Matching Green to High Laver out of respect. In 1814 Benjamin[3] Braine was presented with a cup by John Archer Houblon, the Master, the squire of Great Hallingbury and a descendant of Jacob Houblon, the first Governor of the Bank of England.

---

[2]The Petts family were well-established in Hatfield Broad Oak, Sheering and Matching. Edward Petts owned Stock Hall in the 1850s. There is a remarkable incident in 1789 when John Petts of Matching Green sold his wife and two children to John Crab, also of Matching Green. She was paraded three times around the Green with a halter around her waist with about a hundred people watching and afterwards there was music and dancing. It is not known if John, if at all, was related to Ann.

The inscription reads –

This Cup was presented to
Benjamin Braine Quare Esq.,
of Matching Green
in the County of Essex
by John Archer Esq.,
Member of the County,
Henry John Conyers Esq.,
And Members of the Essex Hunt,
In testimony of their sense of his zeal
In promoting their sport,
And his polite attention on all occasions.
25th November, 1814.   John Nesbitt, Sec.

The Quare Cup

In 1831 the artist Dean Wolstenholme Snr painted a set of four pictures of the Essex Hunt. One was of Manwood which was owned by Tudor Henry, and then later by his nephew, Tudor Brain. Another was of the opening meet at Matching Green. All the figures in this second picture, including the hounds and horses, are portraits. We know from *The Essex Foxhounds* book who is in the picture, but not which portrait is which. Henry and Tudor[1] Quare are there, and an indication of which ones they are can be taken from the fact that, with T.D.Ridley, a brewer from Chelmsford, they are in green coats. This set of pictures was very popular, and Dean Wolstenholme and his son, also called Dean, painted a number of editions which, interestingly, vary in detail. Also, the pictures were engraved and these adorn many an Essex country house.

The Start of the Hunt at Matching Green, 1831, by Dean Wolstenholme Snr, engraved by Dean Wolstenholme Jnr. Tudor and Henry Quare will be two of the three riders wearing green coats. The large house on the far left behind the trees is *The Limes* where Henry Quare lived.

Another version of the Matching Green picture

Gone to Ground at Man Wood, with a View of Hatfield Broad Oak beyond
painted by Dean Wolstenholme Jnr, 1831.
Manwood was owned by Henry Quare and then his nephew, Tudor.

Another version of the picture of Manwood

It is interesting to note the considerable difference in detail between the pictures. The rule of thumb that experts use to distinguish the work of the father from that of the son is that Dean the elder favoured dark skies and leafy trees while his son favoured blue skies and leafless trees. This does not help very much in identifying the artist in our examples, as there are pictures with blue skies and leafy trees, and dark skies and leafless trees!

Marianne Quare, widow of Benjamin[3], the surgeon, died in 1833. She left her grand piano to her daughter Elizabeth and some silver castors to her daughter Marianne, whose second husband was the Reverend John Hayden, vicar of Swanlands, Yorkshire. The Quare cup went to her son Henry. Of the next generation Daniel[4] had one son, Daniel[5], who lived from 1784 to 1848. Benjamin Braine[3] had eight surviving offspring: Justinian, Henry Thomas, Jacob Hewitt, Tudor Brain, Alfred Brain and Benjamin Brain[4], and two girls, Elizabeth and Marianne. Benjamin Braine[4] lived at Maytrees House, Matching Green, which later became the village shop. Justinian left the land and became a stockbroker, as did his brother Jacob and sons Horace and Arthur. Arthur's son Lionel, who worked in insurance, in 1959 bequeathed to the Clockmakers' Company his signet ring. The ring had the motto, *Facta non Verba*, which translates as *Deeds not Words*.

Image courtesy of the Worshipful Company of Clockmakers

Arthur Quare's signet ring

Lionel stated that he was the last direct descendant of Daniel[1], which clearly was wrong as he had numerous cousins living, the descendants of Tudor Brain. He may have lost touch with these relations.

Tudor Brain lived at Kingstons, a fine farmhouse in Matching. He took over this property in the following way. On the 1841 census he is living, aged 38, possibly in *The Limes*, with his brother Henry and sister, Elizabeth. At Kingstons we find William Brown, 40, farmer, together with Ann West, 45, and Mary West, 20, both of independent means. The Tithe award for the period has William Brown occupying the property, with J.T.Selwin, Lord Rookwood's father, as owner. In 1845, Tudor marries Mary West. Interestingly, her full name is Mary Ann Quare West and she is the daughter of Timothy West, a coal merchant from Lambeth. It is not clear what her earlier Quare connection is. Sadly, Mary dies in 1848 aged 28, leaving Tudor with two young children, Ernest, two, and little Alethea, only three months. He never marries again. Tudor farmed out little Ernest with the Read family on Matching Green. They already had two children his age. Alethea lived with her grandmother, Ann West, also on the Green. Ten years later Alethea is living with her Uncle Henry at *The Limes* and Ernest is back with his father at Kingstons, presumably when not at school, helping with the farm. Tudor is recorded at Kingstons, a widower, farming 147 acres with six men and two boys. He would have taken over the tenancy from William Brown, and it remained in Quare hands until Ernest gave it up in 1886.

Tudor was both a farmer and a maltster. Life could be hard for the labouring classes at the time he was farming. In 1845 Joshua Redington, aged 57, was arrested for stealing three faggots from Tudor which were stored at Manwood. Tudor's employee, George Walker, saw Joshua pick up the faggots, and he had only gone a few yards when he was stopped. In court his barrister, Charles Gray, was not much help. He admitted that the case against Joshua was so strong that he was at a loss to suggest any grounds on which he could be acquitted. He was found guilty and the Governor of Colchester gaol reported previous convictions, the most recent being in 1831. The Chairman of the Quarter Sessions said that in consideration of his age and the time passed since the last conviction, he would not have him deported, but he sentenced him to twelve months' hard labour. A few years later William Reed, who had been employed on the farm for thirty years, was given an award of twelve shillings and sixpence by the Agricultural and Labourers' Friendly Society. At the time, a loaf of bread cost eight pence so his reward was better than nothing, but not very generous after thirty years.

Henry has interests in Maltings in Harlow, Matching and Sawbridgworth and lived at *The Limes*; indeed he may have built it. We give here an account of a robbery from Tudor and Henry's Harlow maltings.

The Great Harlow Malt Robbery

In 1842 Tudor[1] and Henry Quare were in partnership as maltsters, and in August of that year they were robbed of 76 bushels[3] and three quarters of a peck of malt from their maltings in Harlow. Two brothers, Joshua, 18, and George Patmore, 21, sons of a farmer from Start Hill, Birchanger, Bishop's Stortford and David Lincoln, 56, their employee, were arrested for the felony. To start with there was a hearing in front of the Magistrate in Epping. The court was crowded with local maltsters and farmers from all over the neighbourhood – there having been a number of similar robberies recently. Then the case moved to Chelmsford quarter sessions. Tudor[1] was the first to give evidence. He stated that he lived with his brother Henry and they were maltsters in Sawbridgeworth and Matching. Also, he rented No. 6 Malting at Harlow from Richard Barnard a farmer and maltster and a collateral ancestor of the current owner of Stock Hall. On Sunday 7th August he had rather more than 300 quarters of unscreened brown malt stored in No. 6. It had been made up by John Shipton, his maltster, and carted to Harlow by John Burr. The next day he was told that the maltings had been broken into and ten quarters[4] were missing. John Burr then gave evidence and confirmed these quantities. Seth Salman, one of Tudor's employees, reported that on the Monday morning he passed by the Harlow maltings and saw the tracks of a cart leading to and from the buildings. Tudor told him to follow the tracks. James Branch, Richard Barnard's watchman, reported that on the 7th all was secure but by the next morning Tudor's maltings had been broken open and there were tracks to and from the yard. Richard Barnard confirmed this and stated that he sent for a policeman. Constable William Richardson reported that he came to the scene, viewed the tracks and also the hoof prints, one made by a half-shoe and the other of a shoe of a peculiar shape. He traced the wheels towards Epping and came across a cart, heavily laden with sacks, being driven by David Lincoln. When he asked Lincoln what his load was, he replied that he did not know. Then he asked if the load was malt and Lincoln replied that he believed it was. Richardson then arrested him and he told the policeman that his master was George Barker Patmore, whose name was on the side of the cart. His instructions had been to go on the London Road where he would meet Joshua Patmore at the corner of Redricks Lane. This he did. Joshua took the cart off to Harlow on his own and he met up with him again, the cart now loaded, at the railway

---

[3] A bushel is a measure of capacity and equal to eight gallons or 36.4 litres. There are four pecks to a bushel.
[4] A quarter is a quarter of a pound or 4 ounces.

bridge. Joshua instructed him to drive the cart to London. Richardson then took the horse and cart to Epping and secured them at his premises there. He measured the wheels and found they exactly met the impressions on the ground. Then, with Superintendent Thomas Godwin and Lincoln he went to *The Imperial Brewers* public house in Whitechapel where Lincoln pointed out George and Joshua Patmore. Lincoln told the brothers that he had got into trouble with the malt. George replied that this was impossible as the horse, cart and malt were his. Joshua said he knew nothing about any of it, but the brothers were arrested. On returning to Epping, Richardson examined the malt and took samples, which he produced in court. Aaron Barltrop, a blacksmith, then gave evidence about the horseshoes. Superintendent Godwin collaborated Richardson's evidence and added that he found a broken horseshoe at the bottom of the cart. John Shipton, Tudor's maltster, disposed that he made the malt at Matching Green. He compared a sample from the cart to one from the maltings and they matched exactly, both being made with this barley with red ends. James Foster, the publican of *The Crown* in Market Street just across the lane from the maltings, confirmed that on Sunday morning he saw Joshua who asked him about a room. Elizabeth Barnes of Thremhall turnpike reported that Joshua Patmore and David Lincoln passed through her turnpike in a cart. Rowland Mardell, a publican of Hallingbury, stated that David Lincoln had a pint of beer in his pub on the 7th. William Campbell, a policeman, while on his Start Hill beat, and in conversation with Patmore's sister near their house, saw a man with an empty cart leaving their yard. He later saw Lincoln in Ilford gaol and believed him to be the same man. William Gant, a porter at Harlow station, reported that Joshua bought a ticket to London on Monday morning. He looked tired, as if he had been up all night and his shoes were dirty.

One or two questions arise here. If Joshua passed through the Thremhall turnpike, he was going the wrong way. Also, did not Joshua have an accomplice when loading up the malt? It is unlikely one man could have made up 17 sacks and load them onto a cart in the middle of the night. The likelihood is that he did, but the brothers kept quiet about him and he was never apprehended.

With such a weight of evidence provided by a highly professional police force, the defendants did not stand much of a chance. Also, it was unwise to carry out a robbery with your name emblazoned on the side of your cart, and a horse with easily identifiable hooves. Mr Knox, the defending barrister, did his best by producing two farmers from Birchanger as character witnesses, but it was of no avail. The jury were out for only a short time and returned a verdict of guilty for all three. Mr Round, the chairman, passed a sentence of ten years' deportation.

Joshua was deported to Bermuda which, on the face of it, would sound a good destination, but he was held in the hulk *Hamilton*, and only let out to work on the construction of the dockyard. However, he escaped but was recaptured, and this time was sentenced to deportation for fifteen years to Tasmania. He travelled there via London on the *Pestonjee Monajee*, arriving in Hobart in February 1847. He prospered in Australia working as a labourer, servant and overseer at various stations in Tasmania. He received his ticket to leave in 1853, which meant he was on probation and virtually a free man, and married Maria Gangell. They had eight children, one of whom lived until 1945. In 1880 his third son, also Joshua, was married. In the announcement in *The Hobart Mercury* the father is described as Mr Joshua Patmore of Sandy Bay, a fashionable suburb of Hobart, so it looks as if he was well-established. He died in 1893 aged 61. There is no information on David Lincoln. 56 is not a good age to start a new career as a convict in Australia, especially if you were the fall guy. The fate of George is a bit more difficult to follow. He must also have been deported but we next find him back in England in 1855, implicated in a series of burglaries. In the reports he is described as a tall stalwart-looking man and a 'transport'. He was arrested and remanded on flimsy evidence and must have been found not guilty. He would have served his time in Australia and come home because Joshua sent for the family and they embarked on *The Indian Queen* in 1856, paying £121 for their tickets. The party consisted of George, his sister and two brothers and his parents, but George died on the voyage out.

Little Laver Hall Farm, which later was called Little Laver Grange,
was occupied by Henry Quare in 1847

In the Post Office directory for 1874, four Quares are listed: Ernest, Daniel[6], a farmer, Henry Thomas, a farmer, and Tudor Brain, a farmer and maltster. Daniel[6] was the son of Daniel[5] and was born in Shoreditch and christened there at St Leonard's. In 1847 Henry Thomas owned or rented at various times Little Laver Hall, Manwood Green and Stone Hall farms. In 1855 James Trundle, a 25 year old labourer employed by Henry, together with Thomas Byatt, 44, stole a live sheep from Henry at Manwood Green Farm. Henry's shepherd was counting the sheep and found one missing. He was suspicious as another of Henry's men, Patmore, had found a sheepskin in a nearby field and traces of blood and entrails were also found. Footmarks led to James's lodgings and when the police searched Thomas Byatt's house they found a bag containing fat and pieces of mutton which matched the fleece. When arrested, Thomas asked if he would be deported. In fact, at that time the sentence could be death but in the end each of them were sentenced to one year's hard labour.

Tudor's Maltings at Matching painted by Augustus John in 1905.
They were larger, as can be seen in the Wolstenholme picture of
the Green in 1832 and in the 1885 sketch on the cover

Alfred[1] Brain, 1811-1872, and his sons lived a peripatetic life and graduated from being farmers to gentlemen of leisure. In 1841, aged 30, we find him living at Watermans End[5] and described as a farmer, with his wife Martha, 27, two daughters, Martha, 5 and Jane, 3, and three servants.

Watermans End Farmhouse later on in the Century

In 1851 he has moved to Walnut Tree House, Widford, Hertfordshire, eight miles away. The description column on the census forms is headed, *'Profession, Trade, Employment or of Independent Means'*. Alfred[1] now enters descriptions that show he is of independent means and for 1851 there is recorded, *'Income from houses'*. He has six children: Jane, 12, Caroline, 11, Rosa, 7, Alice, 6, Herbert, 4, and Alfred[2], one month. There was also one servant. Jane and Herbert are recorded as being born in Thorley so they may have lived there for a while. We next find him in 1871 living at 2 Gordon Terrace, Holland Road, Lambeth with his income coming from *'landed property'*. Besides his wife Martha he had Herbert, 24, Jane, 33, Rosa, 27 and one servant living with him. Herbert is described as having no occupation. Alfred[1] dies the next year in Lambeth. In 1881 we find Herbert and Alfred[2] living at 174 Grafton Street, Marylebone Street, both unmarried and described as gentlemen. Herbert dies three years later aged 37. In 1891 Alfred[2] is

---

[5] Where the author now lives.

living at Mary Manton's Lodging House at 73 Grand Parade, Brighton, described as *'living on means'*, and two years later he marries Mary Brown in Cookham, Berkshire, but he does not enjoy married life for long as he dies the next year – but not before a son is born, Herbert Alfred Braine, in 1894. Herbert will have been named after his late uncle and father and also has the family name, Braine, with the old-fashioned spelling. Mary marries again in 1905 to a stockbroker, Edgar Stephens. Herbert is educated at Marlborough College and is shown in the school register as the son of the late A. Quare and in the care of E.P. Stephens, his stepfather, of Taplow Priory, Bucks. He has a distinguished military career, joining the Royal Munster Fusiliers in 1914, aged 20, being wounded, mentioned in dispatches three times and winning the Military Cross and the Croix de Guerre. He finishes the war as a Major and retires in 1922. He is in uniform again in the Second World War and is recorded as a Major in 1944 travelling out to Aden, Egypt and Uganda. He dies in 1976 aged 80.

Daniel[6] married Mary Lake of High Laver, and the 1841 census records him as living at Manwood Green. He had three children, one of whom, Alfred[3], became a wheelwright. He served his apprenticeship with Joseph Corton of Billericay and then set up business at Radley Green which is in the parish of Willingale Doe, where his great great grandfather Daniel[4] had been a landowner. The 1845 Tithe Redemption shows that Daniel[4] owned some 35 acres around Walls Green, next door to Radley Green, so that must be the reason Albert[3] settled there; indeed, adjacent to Walls Green is Quires Green, which may be a corruption of Quare and so named because the family were landowners. Alfred[3] married twice and had seven daughters and one son. Four of his daughters and his second wife were schoolteachers. He died aged 87 in 1918.

Indeed, the Quare family were a formidable force in Education in the Radley Green area. It all started when James King took over as Master of Highwood School in 1865. On his first day he only had six pupils but he soon got the numbers up. Many pupils would play truant in August to help with the harvest and also in October when they could pick blackberries at a shilling a peck. Two years later his wife joined him as assistant mistress. Two pupils then were Lydia and Ellen Quare, Alfred[3]'s daughters. In 1870 Mrs King was expecting so she enlisted her 23-year old sister, Francis Sheppard, to help. In 1871 Alfred[3]'s wife died and a year later, when he was 41 and she 25, he married Francis and the next year she was appointed headmistress of the new Radley Green school, where she presided for 25 years. She raised standards and one mother complained that her eleven year old was 'too young for arithmetic'. In 1872, aged 15, Lydia was made a monitor and started as a pupil-teacher, a system by which the older pupils taught the younger ones. Later on, her sisters Ellen and Charlotte became pupil-teachers. In 1896, aged 62, Francis died. Her youngest daughter, Mabel, was in the school at the time and became a monitor and later a teacher. Lydia, then 39, took over the post of headmistress, a post she held for 26 years. She always received excellent reports and on retiring at the age of 66 she continued as one of the school managers[6].

Daniel[6]'s second son, Daniel[7] Linley, died aged two. His daughter, Mary Worriker, was born in Little Laver, and in 1860 married Charles Blyth, who farmed 100 acres at Elm Farm on the High Laver side of Matching Green with four men and one boy. It is interesting that while Mary came from Little Laver and Charles from High Laver, they were married at St. Leonard's, Shoreditch. The Quare family must have had a special relationship with that church. Mary had a child every second year until she had seven. They retired to Newport, Essex, where Mary died aged 91 and Charles aged 87. They were married for 77 years. In fact, longevity runs in the family as her brother Alfred lived until he was 87. Mary's second name, Worriker, is interesting because her great grandfather Daniel[4] mentions in his will of 1831 that his property of Warden's Hall, Willingale was inherited from Thomas Worriker. No doubt this was a significant event and the family wanted to note it. Two interesting points arise about Albert[3] the wheelwright. Firstly, why did he take up this craft rather than become a farmer like his father? He was an only surviving son and there was land to take over. Perhaps he had inherited an instinct for craftsmanship from his forbears? The other question concerns the mystery of his first marriage. A certificate exists, dated 1856, stating that an Alfred Quare Blows, a wheelwright aged 26, the son of Daniel Blows, a farmer, married Eliza Carter, aged 29, in Croydon Parish Church. This must be Alfred and Eliza, his first wife, as so many facts fit with information from other sources, but why adopt the surname 'Blows'? Also there are records of three births and one death for Chelmsford for Frederick Quare Blows, born and died 1861, Charlotte Quare Blows, born 1865 and Laura Quare Blows, born 1866, but after 1866 the name Blows is abandoned. There is no logical explanation for all this. His father-in-law was a labourer so perhaps the marriage was opposed by the family, but this is not too plausible. There is a Blows Green and Blows Farmhouse very close to Love's Green where Alfred[3] settled but it is difficult to see a connection. The question remains a mystery.

Ernest had a long life, living from 1847 until 1936. He was a good-looking, well-built athletic man with mutton-chop whiskers, and can be considered the last of the male line of Quares of Matching. At first he lived at Hazeldene Lodge, now called Lascelles Lodge, and then moved to the larger Honington House, which he probably built, as it

---

[6] Information on these schools is to be found in *Educating Writtle and Nearby – School Days and Childhood Memories* published by Writtle Archives in 2010.

does not appear on the maps until shortly before he moved there. The 1881 census recorded him as being a farmer of 322 acres. He attended the *Royal Agricultural College,* Cirencester, for whom he played cricket. The 1871 census has him living at Honington, Lincolnshire, as an agricultural pupil to George Sills, an owner of 683 acres employing nine men and four boys. He must have liked the village as he named his house after it. He married Elizabeth Coultas, the daughter of a prosperous ironmonger and timber merchant from Grantham, in 1872, and they had four children.

In 1886, his lease having run out, Ernest sold his stock at Kingstons and Manwood farms. Sir Henry Selwin Ibbotson, later Lord Rookwood, took the farm in hand with George Britton as bailiff. Tudor, now 79, went on living there until he died three years later. The sale particulars are interesting as they give an insight into the involvement of a Victorian farmer. Here they are:

- 12 Powerful Drought Horses (Mostly Young)
- 23 1½ and 2 year-old Shorthorn Steers and Heifers
- 1 Cow and Calf
- 3 Barreners *(A Cow not in calf for the year)*
- 15 Calves
- Swine and Poultry
- 5 Wagons
- 10 Carts
- Reaping and Mowing Machines
- Cultivator, Ploughs, Harrows, Drills, Rolls, Haymaker, Dressing Machine, Horse Drag, Chaff-Cutter, Barn tackle, Cart and Plough harnesses.
- Numerous other effects for the cultivation of 350 acres of land.

Ernest was 39 at the time and no doubt he could have renewed the lease, but perhaps he was reducing his farming interests to free up time for hunting. He was a renowned hunting man and can be seen in a picture of the meet at the *Green Man*, Harlow. Indeed, he had good reason for his keenness in the field. In 1880 *The Essex Newsman* reported:

Voracious Fox at Ongar

During the last few days some 40 young ducks, the property of Mr Ernest Quare, have disappeared from his farm at Matching Green. Inquiry has proved that the thief was a fox. The remains of several of the ducks were found in a ditch, and a fox has been seen taking some of his victims away.

R. Lockwood   R. T. Grubb   J. Pelly   E. Quare   W. Single   W. S. Horner
    W. Sewell   E. S. Bowlby   G. Buxton

The Meet at the Green Man, Harlow on March 17 1894[7]

---

[7] John Pelly, whose groom sent his guest's hunter to the knacker's yard by mistake, see footnote on page 52, is to the right of the grey.

Illustrated above are two pictures of Hazeldene Lodge. It is not known if the
family on the coach are the Quares. The house had the reputation of being
haunted and the picture has a rather ethereal feel to it.

Honington House, incorrectly captioned in this post card, was a more substantial house than Hazeldene Lodge. It was bombed in World War II and then rebuilt.[8]

Honington House from the back after the bombing

---

[8] This post card which was sent on 26th June 1913 by B.H. of 37 Park Avenue, Chelmsford to A.T. Tomes of Ashbourne Grove, East Dulwich, contains two moves from a postal chess game, Pawn to Bishop's 3 and Rook to Queen 1.

In *Leaves from a Hunting Diary*, Ernest is often recorded as out hunting with one or more of his daughters, Elizabeth, Brisies and Marianne. Harry Yerburgh describes him as a popular man and an enthusiast. 'Jorrocks' in *The Sporting Gazette* of December 1880 reported on a hunt at Hatfield, when firstly Lord Rookwood, the Master, was thrown into a brook by his horse and then, 'Only the earnest entreaties of numerous friends prevented the resolute horseman Mr Ernest Quare from charging an enormous gate, nailed and strongly bound with iron'. From 1892 he kept a pack of beagles and won a number of prizes at the Peterborough show, including the Championship Cup in 1899 with Stormer. Stormer was a very celebrated hound. Not only does he feature in *Leaves from a Hunting Diary* but he had a write-up in *Country Life*. He was described as having plenty of substance and a good neck and shoulders. With his kennelmate, *Scalper*, he won the Couples Competition, and the *Country Life* correspondent remarked that *Scalper* was an even finer hound. However, he never had his photo taken and one hopes he was not put out.

Stormer, winner of the Champion Cup at Peterborough in 1899

MR. E. QUARE'S STORMER.

Stormer as he appeared in *Country Life*

One of Ernest's daughters out riding.
We know the name of the horse, *Flyer*, but not the name of the daughter

One of Ernest's daughters outside Hazeldene Lodge

Ernest's harriers at a Meet
at George Hart's Farm, Thornwood Common, 1896

In 1896 he bought a twenty-couple pack of harriers from Edward Barclay, the Master of the Puckeridge. He employed William Maiden as a Kennel Huntsman and First Whip at the kennels at Honington House. At a meet of the Harriers at Matching in 1896 Ernest was presented with a silver hunting horn by Salvin Bowlby, the Master of the Essex Foxhounds, on behalf of the subscribers to the harriers. Afterwards there was a champagne breakfast for between 60 and 70 people.

MR. QUARE'S HARRIERS.

THE accompanying illustrations are of an Essex pack of harriers belonging to Mr. Ernest Quare, which were taken on the occasion of a meet at Beech Hill Park, the residence of Mr. A. J. Edwards.

Unfortunately the day was a very bad one for the purposes of photography, and of some eight or ten plates used in the bad light and incessant rain, only the two pictures here given were reproduceable.

Mr. Quare's harriers were originally the property of the late Mr. E. E. Barclay, and were purchased by Mr. Quare on Mr. Barclay taking the Mastership of the Puckeridge fox-hounds. They are a very smart, well-bred, level lot of hounds, many of them prize-winners at the Peterborough Harrier Show.

The kennels are at Matching Green, near Harlow. Mr. Quare hunts on the average five days a week over the same country as the Essex foxhounds. He has had capital sport this season; as, indeed, has been the general experience with harrier packs throughout the country. The weather being so unpropitious accounts for the small size of the field on the day that our illustrations were taken; but, as a matter of fact, congested fields are very much the exception with this pack.

Mr. Quare is a very practical Master of harriers, and while he takes care to see that a certain number of kills give his hounds blood, has avoided the error into which so many who lack the patience necessary to make a good huntsman are apt to fall—to wit increasing the standard height of his hounds. His harriers do not run much over 16½ inches taken all round, which

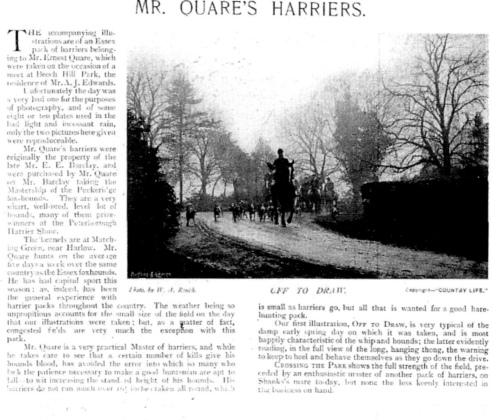

Photo. by W. A. Rouch.   OFF TO DRAW.   Copyright—"COUNTRY LIFE."

is small as harriers go, but all that is wanted for a good hare-hunting pack.

Our first illustration, OFF TO DRAW, is very typical of the damp early spring day on which it was taken, and is most happily characteristic of the whip and hounds; the latter evidently reading, in the full view of the long, hanging thong, the warning to keep to heel and behave themselves as they go down the drive.

CROSSING THE PARK shows the full strength of the field, preceded by an enthusiastic master of another pack of harriers, on Shanks's mare to-day, but none the less keenly interested in the business on hand.

Photo. by W. A. Rouch.   CROSSING BEECH HILL PARK.   Copyright—"COUNTRY LIFE."

**Ernest's harriers were given a full page in *Country Life*
for April 1897**

**Ernest, centre, surrounded by fellow cricketers,
perhaps in the garden of Honington House**

The above photo was in all probability taken at the match between Lord Rookwood's XI and Ernest's XI, played at Matching Green in August 1898. *The Chelmsford Chronicle* gave a colourful description of the scene and faithfully recorded the scores. The match was to become an annual affair with the winning captain taking away the cup presented by Lady Rookwood, but no record of any subsequent matches can be found.

Details of the background of the players are found in appendix 1.

GRAND MATCH AT MATCHING GREEN.

LORD ROOKWOOD'S XI. v. MR. E. QUARE'S XI.,

FOR LADY ROOKWOOD'S CUP.

A grand cricket match was played at Matching Green between elevens selected by the Right Hon. Lord Rookwood, captained by Capt. Calverley, and Mr. Ernest Quare, M.B. Lady Rookwood presented a handsome silver cup to be played for annually, and to be held by the captain of the winning team during the year. The conditions also contain the proviso that on the cup being won by either team a certain number of times the cup will become the property of the captain. Good cricket was shown during the match, the batting of Mr. Howard Fowler being especially noticeable. Corben James, G. Tossetti, and B. Cornell also handled the bat in good style, and, as an old resident said, "such cricket has not been played on Matching Green for many years." The fielding on both sides was smart, and Captain Calverley and his merry men were kept busy for a long time by Mr. Tossetti, but at last the gallant Captain reformed his men, and seeing the batsman's weak point himself went into the slips, with the result that in a few minutes the ball was placed in his hands.

The captain's smart catch, following on his well-laid tactics, received the loud applause of the spectators. Eventually, however, Mr. Quare managed to secure the brush.

The game was watched by Lady Rookwood and the home party from Down Hall, and about 200 of the neighbouring gentry. Both teams were entertained at luncheon in a marquee on the ground by Lord Rookwood, Mr. Joseph Thurgood, of Harlow, catering. Score :—

Ld. ROOKWOOD'S XI.		Mr. QUARE'S XI.	
P. Loraine, b Tossetti	4	D. Tossetti, b Loraine	2
W. Barnet, b Tossetti	3	W. Corben, b Loraine	21
Dr. White, b Tossetti	7	James, lbw, b Day	35
Howard Fowler, c D. Tossetti, b James	56	G. Tossetti, c Calverley, b White	42
W. Day, b Tossetti	3	P. Cornell, b Day	34
J. Bonham-Carter, b Cornell	16	C. Wright, c and b Keeley	6
C. Fane, c Saville, b Cornell	10	A. Cornell, b Day	4
F. N. Day, b Fane	3	E. Quare, l b w, b Loraine	3
A. Keeley, c Cornell, b James	0	M. Tyndale-White, b Loraine	3
F. Scott, b James	0	J. Saville, b Loraine	1
Capt. Calverley, not out	0	T. Quare, not out	0
Extras	17	Extras	11
	119		160

The umpires were Lord Rookwood and F. C. Larter.

The report of the cricket match in *The Chelmsford Chronicle* of 19.8.1898

Ernest was an excellent all-round cricketer. Besides playing for *Cirencester Agricultural College* he turned out for Matching Green, North Essex and Moor Hall. The latter team was under the patronage of John Parry Watlington of Moor Hall, Harlow. The site of

Moor Hall is just on the other side of the motorway on the Old Harlow–Matching road. It was taken over by the army during the war. They used the cellars for exploding detonators, and all that now remains is a lodge and a gate.

In 1866 Ernest, along with Herbert Rhodes, Cecil Rhodes's brother, also played for Bishop's Stortford against an All England XI. Bishop's Stortford were allowed 18 men in their team, presumably because the All England team were so strong. This handicap was finely judged as the result was a tie, each side scoring 261 runs. Ernest also played for Lincolnshire and Shropshire. He was selected for the inaugural match of the Essex County Cricket Club in 1876 between the Gentlemen and Players. In the end he did not play but on the other side was Frank Silcock who came from a remarkable Matching family of both cricketers and harness-makers and saddlers. The Silcocks's cottage is still there on Matching Green, next door to Maytrees. It is now called *Saddler's Cottage*. The shop window, although altered, is still there and inside there is a glass-fronted cabinet left over from the saddlery days. Frank lived on the High Street in Ongar where, besides saddlery, he sold cricket equipment. He played for both Essex and Hertfordshire, as did his cousin Joseph who ran a saddlery business on Matching Green. Another brother, Frederick, was also a good cricketer. The business was still going in the nineteen thirties. It is interesting to note that there is a tradition in English village cricket that teams are made up from all social classes. During the French Revolution, while the French peasants were decapitating their aristocracy, the Earl of Winchelsea was playing cricket with his farm labourers.

Ernest was involved in an interesting episode in 1889. He was taking care of a valuable St. Bernard's dog for a friend who lived in Bedford. The animal escaped, and he assumed it had set off for Bedford and he advertised for its recovery. In fact it had gone to Chelmsford, 14 miles away, and settled down in a summer house owned by a Mr T Hellen of New London Road. Mr Hellen tried to persuade it to leave but it just growled at him. To the rescue came two policemen, Inspector Terry and Sergeant Peters who took it to the Shire Hall. A telegram was sent to Ernest who came to retrieve the dog, which answered to the name of *My Lord* and he paid a reward to Mr Hellen of £2.

My Lord was not the only lost animal to come to Matching. In April 1891 a yellow Turbit pigeon with stud and conference rings and a numbered ring on his leg landed at Honington House. He was still there in June when Ernest advertised for his owner to come and claim him.

Ernest was a public-spirited citizen serving as a Churchwarden with Lord Rookwood of Down Hall. He was elected as a member of the Board of Guardians but got into trouble for not attending meetings. He organised a party for the village to celebrate the Queen's jubilee in 1887. Every cottage received a substantial piece of beef. Lunch was served to all the parishioners at Honington House, after which about 400 people assembled on the Green to listen to a band and to watch sports, which included sack races, donkey races and a married-woman's race. This last race had to be run twice to console those who did not win the first time. After the sports Mrs Quare kept open house to all and at 9.30 pm there were fireworks. Two years later, Ernest hosted a school treat for all the Sunday school children. There was a substantial tea and then amusements in the back field including swings, coconut-throwing and an Aunt Sally. In an era when hierarchy was important Ernest, after Lord Rookwood, was the second man of the village.

The Quare family received a bonus when Hugh Dawson Raincock, a retired stockbroker, died in 1878 without any children and left £102,000 about £10 million in today's money. Elizabeth Quare, Benjamin[3]'s daughter, was his first wife and she died in 1856. Three years later he married Mary Hart, sister of George Hart of North Weald Place, a keen hunting man who was often out with the Essex, whose farm is illustrated on page 43. George's father and brother farmed Housham Hall Gate farm in Matching until the family moved to North Weald. Hugh left £5,000 to his niece, Helen Bokenham, Brisies Quare's mother-in-law. He left £1,000 in trust for Tudor[1], Justinian and Jacob's widow, Marie, and £1,000 to Alfred[3] Brain Quare. £500 went to the children of William Beloe Rix, a cousin and a Doctor who lived at Matching Green. £100 went to his sister, Sophia. He mentioned that she had plenty of money but he did not want her to think he had forgotten her. £1,000 went to *The Fund for Decayed Members of the Stock Exchange*. Almost all of Hugh's fortune was invested in 5% Russian Bonds. It is just as well he died when he did and not in 1916 or it would have all evaporated. A table of all the Quare and Raincock relationships, together with those of the Hewitt family, is shown on sheet four of the family trees. Jacob Hewitt, 1710-1769, a silk merchant of Gracechurch Street, is the patriarch. The most interesting character, besides the millionaire Hugh Dawson, is Captain George Raincock, 1771-1849, a Master Mariner who worked the India route for the East India Company. *HCS Charles Mills* and *HCS Northumberland* were two of his ships. At one time his passengers were so pleased with his seamanship that they put advertisements in the newspapers congratulating him. He was also described as a merchant, an occupation at which he was not much good because in 1815 he went bankrupt. A remarkable number of Raincocks were stockbrokers. In 1913 four of them were listed as members of the Stock Exchange.

The 1901 census shows Ernest living on his own means at Honington House with his wife, two of his three daughters, Brisies, 25, and Marianne, 21, and Tudor[2] his son, aged 23. Also there were Alethea, his 52 year old sister, and two servants, Ellen Sweating and

Sarah Selby. The 1895 *Kelly's Directory* now listed Ernest and his cousin Daniel[6] in the 'Private Residents' section. Before that date they had always been listed in the 'Commercial' section with all the other farmers. This indicated that they were now considered 'gentry'. But this situation did not last for long. Daniel[6] died in 1896 and we will see later on how Ernest fared.

Tudor[2] had enlisted in the Essex Yeomanry and is pictured, mounted outside Honington House, with his Machine Gun troop. In September 1898 he had a lucky escape. He was on holiday at Scratby, near Yarmouth, with his cousins, the Bokenhams. Douglas Bokenham's brother, Laurence, was to later marry Tudor[2]'s sister, Brisies. Douglas and Tudor[2] waded out to a sandbank where a huge wave came and knocked them over. With difficulty Tudor[2] managed to swim ashore but Douglas was lost. He was buried in Matching churchyard.

**Tudor[2], in the uniform of the Essex Yeomanry
outside Honington House, c. 1902**

Tudor[2], bottom left, with the Essex Yeomanry Machine Gun Corps

But clearly Ernest had put too much of his energy into hunting and neglected his other interests, for in 1903 at the age of 56 on a petition of Edward Allcock of Sawbridgeworth, he was declared bankrupt. In May that year there were signs that the wheels were coming off his enterprises. He was fined £5 by the Harlow magistrates for keeping a pack of hounds without a licence. To add insult to injury, at the same session he was fined fifteen shillings for using a carriage without a licence. At a meeting of his creditors at the George Hotel in Bishops Stortford a list of debts was read out. It included –

	£
E.R. Cummings	45
Chaplin and Co, Harlow, Brewers	12
T. Williams	14
Edward Allcock	30
F.M. and T.N. Day, Harlow	15
H. Bowyer, Hatfield Heath	81
Lamont and Warne	18
Miss A. Quare	1,908

H. Nott, Wages	62
J. Trundle[9], Wages	32
W. Reed, Wages	9
J.J. Peacock, Wages	4
Rates	7
T.H.B. Quare	26

His total unsecured debts were £2,613, and £5,260 was secured on Honington House. His only assets were furniture valued at £150. Ernest stated that he had no way of making up the deficit and attributed his downfall to interest on mortgages and the expense of keeping a pack of hounds. It is a pity that Lord Rookwood had died a year earlier[10]. They were fellow churchwardens and he may have been able to help Ernest in his difficulties. At the final hearing liabilities were £7,939 and assets £83. In today's money the liabilities would be about £793,900. Honington was sold to Mr Thomas Welch, a wine merchant. The kennels at Honington House were taken over by the Essex Stag Hounds under the Mastership of Mr Abraham Jackson[11]. The hounds were sold to Mr

---

[9] John Trundle was a member of an extended family of Matching Trundles, a number of whom, but not John, were often in trouble with the law. James Trundle is mentioned earlier when in 1855 he stole one of Henry Quare's sheep. John Trundle in 1905 met a sad end. He was kept on by Alethea as a coachman and was driving a brougham, a four-wheeled coach with an open top for the driver, with a grey horse, along the Matching road when the horse turned round and backed into a ditch. John fell into the road. All this was witnessed by the occupants of a car some 60 yards away belonging to Captain Calverley of Down Hall. They were Ernest Salisbury, the chauffeur to the Captain who had inherited Down Hall from his uncle, Lord Rookwood, two years earlier; Colonel Vyne, and Major Tufnell, whose ancestor appeared in Wolstenholme's portraits of the Essex Hunt. Ernest rescued John, drove him home and then fetched Doctor Day from Harlow, but John died a day or so after. An interesting aspect of this story is that Major Tufnell was Captain Calverley's wife's lover. This couple lived separate lives and the Captain spent most of his time at his houses at Oulton Park, Yorkshire or Chesham Place, London. We do not know what the Major was doing in the Captain's car.

[10] Down Hall, Lord Rookwood's seat, is between Matching and Hatfield Broad Oak where he is buried. The most prominent memorial to him is a pub in Leytonstone which was recently under threat of demolition but has now reopened under the name The Rookwood Village.

[11] Mr Jackson came to an untimely end. He was a prosperous stockbroker from Chelmsford and well-respected in the neighbourhood but he had a hunting accident which set him back and, after six years, he resigned the Mastership. He eventually retired to the Grand Hotel in Northumberland Avenue and became virtually a recluse. On 29 August 1923, aged 67, his body was found floating in the Thames near Rotherhithe Pier. He had drowned but there was a blow to the back of his head. The Coroner at the inquest returned a verdict of 'found drowned', but he did not take into account the blow to the back of the head. Mr Jackson's valet reported that he seemed quite as usual that morning. To this day the circumstances of his death are a mystery.

John Gurney Pelly of Theydon Place[12]. The Quare family moved to 'The Cottage', Matching Green, which is now Wingates. The property had seven rooms and was owned by Alethea and the 1911 census shows her living there together with her sister-in-law, Elizabeth, and one servant. Marianne, her niece, and her husband, Francis Wyndham Grane, were also staying. Ernest is absent. It is not known if he was living somewhere else or just away for the night. Over the next few years the household breaks up. Alethea moves to Nottingham where she dies in 1914. Elizabeth moves to Barnstable, Devon, where she dies in 1924 and Ernest moves to Ipswich, Suffolk, where he dies aged 93 in 1936.

---

[12]John Pelly was a very keen hunting man, often out with the Essex. On one occasion a guest and his horse arrived late one evening for the hunt next day. In the morning the horse was missing. There had been a misunderstanding in the stables and it had been dispatched to the kennels, slaughtered, and fed to the hounds. John Pelly was great great grandfather to Guy Pelly, the friend of Prince William and Harry.

In 1925 Alethea's Executors sell the property to a Mr and Mrs Nimmo, but one mystery remains. In the Quare collection of old photographs there are two of the interior of a small house. On the backs is written:

'Sitting Room at Forge Farm, E. Quare /99'

'Another view of Sitting Room, E.Quare /99'

There is no Forge Farm to be found in the neighbourhood or one with a Quare connection. There is a Forge Cottage next door-but-one to Honington House but Mr Terry Page, the current owner, does not think the photos are of his sitting room. They do fit the sitting room at Wingates but so many alterations have been made over the years that there is nothing to prove this one way or another, and why is 'Forge Farm' written on the back, and if /99 is a date it does not fit because the family moved in 1903? To add to the mystery, there are some 21 photographic portraits and silhouettes along the mantelpiece and shelves. If they are Quares they would be an amazing record, but they are now all lost. Enhanced and enlarged images of some of these are shown.

The sitting room at Forge Farm

Ernest did not live on in Matching for long, and left for Suffolk where he died aged 93 in 1936. Alethea was buried in Matching churchyard. The inscription on her grave was covered with moss but when revealed it reads, *'In loving memory of Alethea Quare who entered eternal life, Dec 7th 1914, aged 68 years'*.

Tudor[2] married Florence Avey, daughter of the landlord of *The King's Head* pub in North Weald. In 1906 they ran *The Vine* pub in Ipswich for a few years before World War I. Two of Ernest's daughters married well. One can see from the photographs of the girls mounted on their horses and ponies that they are both attractive and self-reliant. Brisies married her cousin, Laurence Bokenham, a Doctor, and Marianne married Francis Wyndham Grane, a Surveyor who served as an officer in the Royal Army Service Corps in World War I. Elizabeth did not marry. In the 1901 census she is staying at *The Limes*, just the other side of the Green where three generations of her cousins are living: Maria MacIlwain, 71; her daughter Anna Last[13], 33; and grandson, Hugh Last, 6. Maria is the daughter of Jacob Quare and was the widow of a distinguished surgeon, George MacIlwain[14]. Elizabeth is listed as a 'sick nurse' so no doubt Maria needed looking after. Later on she became a school nurse and health visitor. Anna MacIlwain married William Last, the Director of the Science Museum in Kensington.

Her wedding to William in Matching church in July 1893 was a very fine affair, with her Quare cousins playing prominent roles. As her father had died, (he was 72 when she was born) she was given away by her uncle, Henry Quare. Her train was held by Minnie (Marianne) Quare, who was dressed in white pongee silk, with a white Leghorn hat, trimmed with lace and daises. The reception was at the family home, *The Limes*. The family were generous with their presents: Henry Hewitt gave a hall gong; Ernest and his wife, a dining-room clock; the Misses and Master Quare, bronze Marly horses; Alethea, a silver bread fork; Fanny Quare, silver asparagus tongs; Mr and Mrs Horace Quare, a pair of Princess lamps; and Mrs Daniel Quare[6], a china candlestick. The Raincock cousins gave a case of silver salt-cellars and spoons and an antimacassar.

---

[13]Anna was buried in Matching churchyard. Her memorial reads, 'To the memory of Anna Maria Quare Last, born 3 August 1868, died 2 June 1944, daughter of George MacIlwain, also of her only son, Hugh MacIlwain Last, born 3 December 1894 and died 25 October 1957, and also her only daughter Margaret Gwendolen Last, died 19 May 1986'. In the Matching Parish Records, 1559-1749, there is mention of a vault belonging to the Quare family which is subject to a fee of 20 shillings for every opening. The site of this vault is now unknown but it might be a fine arched unmarked brick one not far from the entrance porch.

[14]George had been married twice before. He married Maria when he was 67 and she 33. He had no surviving children from his previous marriages so must have been delighted when Anna arrived. He died aged 85 in 1882.

Hugh became Camden Professor of Ancient History at Oxford and Master of Brasenose College. During World War II he worked at Bletchley Park. Tudor[2] and Florence had two sons and two surviving daughters, and their descendants are now living on the Essex/Suffolk boarders and in Buckinghamshire.

Enlargements showing the family photos

W. TRUSWELL,   SAWBRIDGEWORTH.

John Trundle, the elderly coachman, with the coach and grey horse
that caused his sad end, in front of Honington House. The lady will be either
Miss Alethea Quare or Mrs Elizabeth Quare.

The Quare Family Trees

The Quare Family Tree

Sheet 1

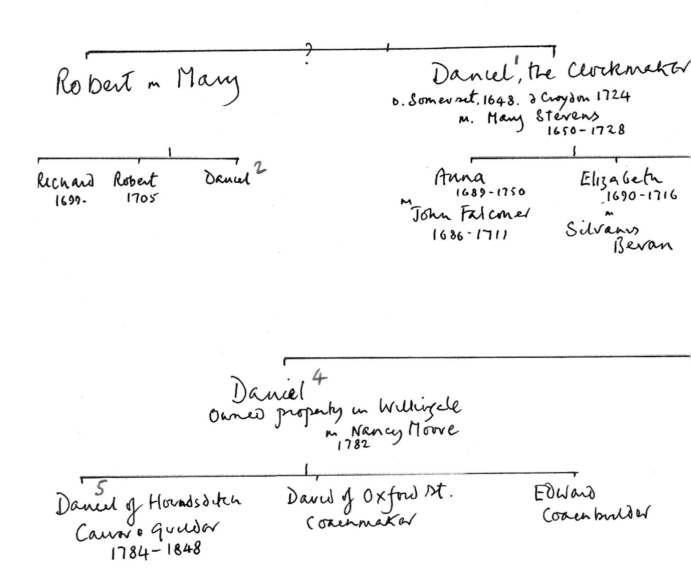

Robert m Mary

Daniel¹, the Clockmaker
b. Somerset, 1648. d Croydon 1724
m. Mary Stevens
1650-1728

Richard
1699-

Robert
1705

Daniel²

Anna
1689-1750
m
John Falconer
1686-1711

Elizabeth
1690-1716
m
Silvanus
Bevan

Daniel⁴
Owned property in Willingale
m Nancy Moore
1782

Daniel of Horndsditch
Canur & guilder
1784-1848⁵

Daniel of Oxford St.
Coachmaker

Edward
Coachbuilder

continued on Sheet 2

58

John Tudor m Anna

Benjamin Brain
Merchant of Tottenham   m   Mary Tudor
Bought Stock Hall
b 1650   Matching

Sarah   Jeremiah   m   Anna Brain   James   Tudor
1690-1717   1683~1729   1686   High Sheriff
m   East India Merchant   of Essex
Jacob Wyan

Benjamin   I   Daniel 3   m   Elizabeth Brain
Brain   1708-1756   b 1707
1710-1716   of Stock Hall

Benjamin Brain 2   James   Mary   Jeremiah
Merchant of Tottenham High Cross   b. Whitechapel
                                                        1732-1765
b. Stepney, 1731 d. Matching 1774
m Ann Petts of Hatfield Broad Oak

Benjamin Brain 3   Ida Lovne
                                         b 1760
1766-1826 Surgeon
?   m Marianne Hewitt
           1767-1833

continued on Sheet 3

59

Daniel [4]
Owned Property in Willingale
M. 1782, Nancy Moore

Daniel [5] of Hornesditch   Danw of Oxford Street
Caun & Gvulder   Coachmaker
1784 - 1848

Daniel [6] 1809 - 1896   Ann
b. Hornesditch. m. Shoreditch, Mary Lett
1841. Living at Manwood Green   of High Laver
                                 1814 - 1895

Alfred Brown [3]   Mary Warricker   Daniel Luley Moore [7]
1831 - 1918   b Little Laver   1852 - 1854
Wheelwright   m 1860, Charles Blyth, Farmer
& Shop Keeper of Radley
M, Eliza   Green.
M2 Frances

Lydia   Eliza   Ellen Jane   Charlotte
School Teacher   School Teacher   1863 - 1935   1865 -
1857 - 1940   1860 -

Edward
Coach Builder

Eliza Ann   Edward Moore   Emma   Ellen Mary   Emily Marie

4 Alfred James.   Elizabeth Frances   Alice Mary   Mabel
Grocer   1876   1878-   School 1881-
1873-1940   Teacher
m Emily

5 Alfred James   Frances Emily
1910-1982   1904-

61

Benjamin Braun Quare [3]
1766-1826   m   Marianne Hewitt
Surgeon   1788   1767-1833

Justinian	Marianne	Henry	Jacob	Elizabeth
1804-1879	Hewitt	Thomas	Hewitt	Braun 1799- 1855
Stockbroker	1791-	Hewitt	1793-1868	m Hugh Dawson
m Harriet Bunn	M, Joseph Webb of Hoveton	1793-1874	Stockbroker	Raincock. Stockbroker
1812-1898	M₂ Revd. John Haydon		m Marie Douglas d 1881	1803-1881

Ada 1842-1931	Horace	Ellen	Fanny	Julia	Walter	Arthur
m. Wⁿ Nash	1836-1922	1838-	1840-1913	1846-1942	1849	1844-1926
1840-1924	Stockbroker	m Stanley Croxton McMurdie 1831-1892		m Edward Wood 1847-		m Maria Clark 1845-1915

Mabel   Lionel Braun
                               1873-1959
                               Insurance Broker
                               Presented seal
                               Ring to Clockmakers'
                               Company.

From Above →
Alfred Braun [1]
1811-1872
of Watermans End & Twyford Mill
m Martha Beaumont

Jane	Caroline	Rosa	Alice	Herbert	Alfred [2]
1839-	1840-	1844-	1845-	1847-1884	1851-1895
m 1879					
Edward Kempe					
Master Mariner					

Herbert Alfred Braun
1884-1968 Royal Munster Fusiliers
m Maud Vans Agnew
1894-1976

Tudor Brain
1806-1889
Farmer & Malster
of Kingstons
Matching
m Mary Ann West
1818-1848

Alfred Brain
1811-1872
m Martha
↓
See below

Benjamin Brain
1789-1855
of Maytrees,
Matching.

Caroline Hewitt
1800-1810

Emma Sophie
1802-1812

Marie Margaret
-1905
m George MacIlwain
Surgeon of The Limes,
Matching

Henry Hewitt
d1904

Helen Douglas
m 1359
Robert Boys
Thomson

Ernest
1846-1936
Master of Harriers
Farmer of
Housham Howe,
Matching
m. Elizabeth Coultas
1351-1924

Alethea
1848-1914

Anna
m Wm Last
1863-1944

Hugh Last
1894-1957

Elizabeth
1373-1956
Nurse

Briseus
1375-1944
M.1909
Laurence Ramcock
Dr. Bokenham
1883-1969

Tudor
Hewitt
Brain
1879-1940
m Florence Avey
1906   1885-1985

Marianne West
1380-1961
m Francis
Wyndam
Grane
1879-1954
Surveyor

Tudor Brain
1912-1996
m Mary Ethel Ledgerwood
1911-2001. b. Lucknow
India

Alethea
1914-1994
m Key

Douglas Ernest
1917-1998
m Sybil Gage
1919-2010

Joan Mary
1919-2008
m Williams

Rosemary
1947-
M Rex Jackson

Bruce
1944
Prof. of Engineering
M, Valarie Musson
M₂ Rita Tail Ayoka

Tudor
1942
m Pamela
Furnell

Jane
m Whitehead 1942-2012

Paul

Peter
m
Selve

Ann
m
Wrighton

Emma
1978

Daniel
1982-
m Natalie

Harriet
1987-

Phoebe
1989-

Charles Tudor
1965-2020

Mathew
1968-
m Eleanor McAneny
1967-

Edward Cameron
1997

63

The Connections of the Raincock, Hewitt, Rix
and Quare Families.

Jacob Hewitt m Mary Cooke
1710-1769   1710-
Silk Mercer   @ St. Ann's, Blackfriars
of Gracechurch St
London

Thomas Hewitt m Sally Taylor
                              M₂ John Rix

Henry Thomas	Emma Sophia	Catherine Elizabeth
	b. Lambeth 1775-1853	1777-1809
	m James Turner Bostock	b. Dulwich
	at Matching	m. 1796 Revd George Rix
		Vicar of Ugley, Essex
		[M₂ Mary Ann Clark
		1789-1843

William Belore Rix	Georgianne Jane	9 Others.
Doctor on Matching Green	1803-1889	
1800-1862		
M Laura Anne Bond		

Hugh Dawson	Harriet	Helen	Mary Dawson	John	Sophia
Raincock	1796	Douglas	1805-1888	Noble	1881-
1803-1881		1800-1828	M		
Stockbroker			Thomas Brandon		
M, Elizabeth Brain			Hemuy. Sol!		
Quare					
1799-1356					
M₂ Mary Hart	Mary Charles Hugh	Albert		Helen Douglas	
1821-1899				M	
Sister of George Hart				Revd Clifton Bokenham	
of North Weald					

Thomas	Douglas	Mary Sheldrake	Mildred	Philip Harold	Dorothy	Laurence
Brandon	Clifton	1876-				Raincock
1872-	1874-1898					D!
	Drowned on holiday					1884-1969
	with the Quares.					m Briscus Quare
	Buried in Matching					
	Churchyard					

John Raincock m Mary Dawson
Lawyer 1739-1790   1740-1798

Marianne   Sally   Ann Dorrington   Henrietta Marie
1767-1883   1765-1765   1707-1342   1771-1836
m Benjamin³   m William Rain Cock   m
Brown   Capt George Raincock
Quare   1771-1849
1766-1826
Surgeon

William   Georgianna   George   John
1804-1849   Harriet   Dawson   Hewitt
m Caroline Clark 1800   b Rickley   1811-1836
                                  1802-1882   Stockbroker
                                  Stockbroker   m Mary Ann
                                  m Martha Hopley

Ellen   Mary   George   Henry   John H   Harry, Naval Architect.
1834-   1835-   1836-1903   m   1838-   Stockbroker   1844
                 Stockbroker   1866   1841-1876   m Caroline Quare
                 m Mary   Catharine   1903
                                 Jones

George   William   Ethel   Harold   Frances   Hugh D   May
1363-   1365-   1370   1375   1332-   1334   1339
         Stockbroker   Stockbroker   Stockbroker

Harry   Laura   Emily   Walter   Florence   Arthur   Martha

Appendix 1

Here is more information, where available, about the characters playing in the Grand Cricket Match on Matching Green in 1898:

Lord Rookwood's XI

Howard Fowler, 1857-1934, was educated at Clifton College where he was captain of the XI. He won a blue at Oxford and also played for Somerset and Essex. He played Rugby Football for Oxford and England.

William and Francis Newcombe Day, born 1877 and 1863, were sons of Doctor Day of Harlow, Ernest's doctor. Francis was a Medical Student.

John Bonham Carter, 1852-1905, was the son of Jack Bonham Carter MP and a member of the distinguished political family.

C. Fane was probably a member of the Fane family of Priors, Brentwood, who produced a number of well-known Essex cricketers.

Captain Horace Calverley, 1862-1922, was Lord Rookwood's nephew and heir.

Ernest Quare's XI

Besides Ernest and his son, Tudor, there were:

Douglas and Gilbert Tosetti were the sons of Max Tosetti, a wine merchant of West Dene, Woodford and Crutched Friars, City of London. Max had an Italian name but was German by birth and was born in Saarbruchen, Prussia, the son of a district clerk. He came to England aged 23 as a shipping agent and later became a prominent importer of champagne. He married Julia, the daughter of William Folks, a vet of Hadham Road, Bishops Stortford and was a keen follower of the Essex Hunt. Both boys were educated at Bancroft's School, Woodford. Gilbert, 1879-1923, played cricket for Essex and in 1902 scored a century for them against Lancashire. In 1905 he was in the team that beat the Australians. He worked in the wine trade with his father and in World War I he served as a Private in the East African Mounted Rifles and died in Kenya in 1923 aged 44. Douglas also played cricket for Essex and was a champagne salesman. In World War I he served as a Major in the Royal Berkshire Regiment and won the MC at the Battle of Loos. He was killed in action on 21.3.1918, aged 39, on the opening day of the German spring offensive. He was much loved by his men and when acting as President of Courts Marshals was, to the annoyance of his superiors, well-known for his leniency. In 1910 the Tosetti family bought a 2,570 acre farm at Uasin Gishu in Kenya and all three were involved in running it. Max died, aged 78, in 1924 having outlived both his cricketing sons.

Walter Corben was a member of the Essex Hunt.

P and A Cornell. George Cornell ran a pub on Matching Green and these two could have been his sons.

Maurice Tyndale-White was the son of Tyndale White of Standon Place, Standon Massey. He was a Lieutenant in the Rifle Brigade.

John Saville, b.1868 was a blacksmith on Matching Green and Ernest's neighbour.

The Umpires were **Lord Rookwood,** 1826-1902, of Down Hall, MP and Financial Secretary to the Treasury and **Police Constable Arthur Larter,** who was stationed at Matching Green.

Appendix 2

Some Account of the Life of Richard Rochead of Edinburgh,
Highwayman, Pirate and Watch-thief.

Robert Rochead, on a Sunday in 1742, held up a coach on Blackheath and stole a Quare watch, No. 569, a gold ring and eight pounds. We know much about Robert because, before they were hung, criminals were encouraged to make a confession of all their sins which was written up and published by the Prison Chaplain. This was not to help the criminal in this life - it was too late for that - but to help him in the next. Also, others would read it and be encouraged to keep on the straight and narrow.

He came from an established family in Edinburgh. The Rocheads owned much of Inverleith, a prosperous suburb, and his father was a merchant. Indeed Robert was such an aristocratic criminal that at times he was known as Sir Robert. He had a good education mastering Latin and Greek and, on leaving school, wishing for an adventurous life, he went to sea. He served an apprenticeship on a ship in the coal trade and did so well that he was promoted to mate. He then served out of Yarmouth in the Dutch trade, but his wanderlust prompted him to come to London where he took up a riotous way of living. When all his money was gone he signed up on the *Anne Galley*, bound for Virginia. On arrival he fell out with the captain and challenged him to a duel. The captain responded by threatening him with gaol. Robert with two others, at the dead of night, then stole a longboat and, pretending they were castaways, sailed up the James River where they were befriended by a planter who sheltered them. A sloop then arrived at the planter's which had had a mate and one hand washed overboard. Robert and his companions, on the planter's recommendation, were taken on. Loaded with tobacco the sloop sailed down the river, and after a while stopped to allow the Captain, a man and a boy to go ashore for provisions. Robert encouraged the ship's company to get drunk and then slipped anchor and headed for the West Indies. After seven weeks they sighted the island of Qualifa-Quaw where the mutinous crew appointed him master. Once on shore he adopted the name of the deposed captain, Captain Ellis, and showed the ship and the cargo to a merchant stating that it was all his. There were three Negro slaves on the ship and Robert promised them all liberty, but he reneged on this undertaking and sold them to a Jewish trader. This was a fateful mistake. One of the Negroes discovered the whole story and exposed him. The new First Mate also turned evidence against him, and he and the other mutineers were thrown in goal. The authorities sent to Virginia for confirmation of the facts. But Captain Ellis had, due to the loss of his ship, died of grief, and the man and boy had sailed for England. There being no one to confirm the mate's evidence, they were all set free.

Robert now sailed for Jamaica where he enlisted as a second mate on a Snow, a square-rigged vessel with two masts, for a buccaneering voyage down the coast to the Bay of Honduras. The trip was going well until, at about 28 leagues off the western tip of Jamaica, they sprung a leak and would have certainly all drowned if they had not been rescued by a turtle-fishing scoop who took all 55 men to Port Royal. He then enlisted as a boatswain on a London-bound ship and arrived with 25 guineas in his pocket, which was enough to set himself up quite well. He then fell in love, and after a few months of courtship they married and had a child. But the money did not last long so he enlisted as a mate on a collier and was doing well there, but the Admiralty issued a rule that any sailor on shore who did not have their protection was vulnerable to a press gang. Indeed he fell victim to such a gang and found himself on board *HMS Cumberland* under Commodore James Stuart as a Foremast Man, where, thanks to the influence of his father, he was promoted to Midshipman and transferred to *HMS Cambridge* under Captain Thomas Wharwood at Spithead, where he was promoted again to Master Mate.

Now it was Robert's turn to join a press gang and he met up with Lieutenant Harrison at *The Golden Lion* at Wapping Stairs. They were to board a tender manned with 16 hands, lying just below, and impress the crew, but Richard, being short of cash, for a consideration, allowed the crew to escape. Over the following weeks he repeated this ruse. Then the story becomes rather confused but it would appear that he changed sides again and set off on a press gang trip on *HMS Neptune* eventually arriving at Leith, the port of Edinburgh, where he met up with his parents and brother, now a distiller. His parents were delighted to see him and he gave his father a valuable collection of clothes and books. The *Neptune* returned to Chatham where Robert obtained leave from the Captain to go to London where he fell into the company of 'lewd women' but could not afford their expenses so once again resorted to his press gang ruse to restore his finances. Things were going well until, while masquerading as a Lieutenant, he press ganged someone who knew him and he was duly arrested and locked up in a tender lying off Tower Wharf. The ship's Captain asked the Admiralty what he should do with him and was told he should be locked up in Marshalsea in irons, where he festered for five months. Luckily, one of the Lords of the Admiralty, Brigadier General Sinclair, knew his father and arranged for him to be posted to the man of war, *HMS Lark*, under Captain Waring.

Just before his capture he had made acquaintance with Sarah Lowther, a pickpocket and forger. Sarah specialised in relieving inebriates of their watches and money and was considered by her fraternity or sisterhood to be a good 'hand' at it. From then on, Sarah was often to support him in time of need.

The *Lark* was to take the new Governor to Jamaica from Spithead, from where Robert wrote to Sarah suggesting she came down, which she did, pretending to be his wife. While waiting for the Governor to arrive they hatched a plot to escape. Sarah procured a Bomboat, a small naval vessel built for carrying mortars. The boat came alongside, the boatman thinking he was on a legitimate trip and they rowed to Gosport where Sarah was waiting with horses. They rode that night to her lodgings in Goldmans Fields, moving on again to King's Head Court, off Shoe Lane, where Sarah resumed her pickpocketing. The next move was to Cooper's Alley, off Whitecross Street, where they lived for about a year. However business fell off so, hoping for better times, they moved back to King's Head Court, but better times did not come. Sarah pawned all her clothes, indeed she hardly had a gown to call her own to go out into the streets. She told Robert he must go as she could not support him. He replied that he would do anything to support her and, prophetically, said he would even venture his neck.

About a week later, he and two other seamen went out on a Saturday night to Goldmans Fields and held up a ship's Captain coming out of a house of ill repute in Ayloffe Street where they robbed him of two guineas, a silver watch and nineteen shillings in silver. The Captain shouted, 'Stop thieves', and a passer-by came to his aid and jumped onto one of the gang. Robert then knocked him over and robbed him of a silver tobacco box, seven shillings in silver and a pinchbeck-headed cane. The gang, each with a cosh in one hand and a pistol in the other, then set off through Whitechapel threatening destruction to anybody who got in their way, and finally made their way back to King's Head Court. Sarah pawned the watch for two guineas and they shared out their gains, Sarah being given a crown for her help, and Robert took the tobacco box at a value of ten shillings. They then retired to a tavern and bought a three shillings bowl of punch to toast their success.

Their good luck continued, for shortly afterwards Sarah picked a pocket for ten pounds which she and Robert proceeded to spend in about a fortnight. For his next venture Robert, with an accomplice, hired two horses and set off down the Chatham Road intending to rob some Navy clerks of the fleet's wages and perhaps some Landlords after the Navy's spending had swelled their coffers. But the fleet was late coming in so they headed back to London, and at Blackheath they met a coach and robbed the occupants of a Quare and Horseman silver watch, No 569, a gold ring and eight pounds. Then they set off to *The Blue Maid* in the Borough and gave a groom a shilling to take the horses back to Smithfield. Robert's next enterprise was a change from highway robbery. He met up with an old shipmate and asked who had recently died. He was told one Robert Roan so he proceeded to forge his will and Sarah took the forgery off to Doctors Commons, pretending to be the widow, to have it proved. Robert hired a chaise, a two-wheeled carriage with an open top, from the landlord of *The Yorkshire Crop* and set off to Chatham to claim Roan's outstanding wages, but someone had got there before him. As happened with crooks, Robert and Sarah fell out and, hearing of a declaration that deserters would be welcomed back, he signed up at *The Black Boy* and *Trumpet* at St Catherine's as a Midshipman on a man of war. He was, however, soon to blot his copybook. A Petty Officer reprimanded him for some offence and he responded by beating him up. The outcome was that he was transferred as a pressed man to *HMS Sunderland* and sent to cruise the Bay of Biscay for two months.

When the *Sunderland* returned to Plymouth, Robert received several letters from Sarah requesting he come up to London. He could not get leave but feigned illness and pretended to visit a Doctor on shore. Sarah sent some money and he headed back to King's Head Court where he joined up with Charles Cleaver, and they took to frequenting *The Van Tromp* in Brick Lane with a view to robbing the landlord. One afternoon, it was very quiet with only an old lady in charge whom they plied with 'hot flip' - a cocktail made of rum, brandy, eggs, molasses and beer, stirred to a caramelized froth with a hot poker. Charles chatted away to her while Robert went upstairs to an escritoire where he stole £150. He then returned downstairs to continue drinking. Then they paid the bill, presumably with the landlord's own money, bid good bye to the old lady and told her that they were off to sea. The next day one of them spent one of the stolen £10 notes in a linen draper's in the City, and the landlord heard about this. Also, three other notes were traced to some Jewish brokers who had bought them at half value. On Sunday 31st December Robert, Walter Nagle and Francis Sherlock met at an inn in Covent Garden and decided, armed with pistols and cudgels and a sword, to go to Wapping. At about 9pm, they accosted a man dressed in a white overcoat and a laced waistcoat, in Wellcose Square. Two of them attacked him and a pistol was put to his head. The third drew a sword and demanded money. The victim, who was slightly inebriated replied, 'Damn my Blood, what do you mean?' To which one of the villains replied, 'Damn my Blood, you dog, your money or your life'. The swordsman joined the chorus, 'Damn my Blood. Why don't you shoot the dog if he does not deliver his money, for we gentlemen are not to be trifled with?' The victim, no doubt bolstered with Dutch courage, ignoring the pistol to his head, replied, 'Shoot Who? Damn my Blood if I have got any money for you.' A rather incoherent reply, but he then had the presence of mind to wrestle out of his hold and make his escape. Richard and his cohorts were not to be put off by this setback, and headed for New Hermitage Stairs, Nightingale Lane in Radcliffe Highway to await another victim. Soon a gentleman, carrying a lantern, and his wife and young son came by. But a press gang emerged from the direction of Plow Alley and distracted the assailants from their task.

Much frustrated, they now resolved to rob the first person they met and set off in the direction of Tower Hill. Shortly afterwards they encountered a pipe-smoking Dutchman whom they ordered to stand still or they would blow his brains out. He submitted and they searched his pockets, finding seven shillings. He did not give up lightly however and produced a knife, but was overpowered. Robert clubbed him with his stick and left him in a sorry condition. The plunder continued. That night they stopped a gentleman in an alleyway near Guildhall and robbed him of a green silk purse containing six half-crowns, nineteen pence, a corkscrew and a pair of tweezers. After this they repaired to *The Anchor and Crown* near Shoe Lane where the loot was divided over a tankard of Bombow, a brew of the time whose constituents are now unknown.

The pillage went on. On Tuesday 3rd January in Brewhouse Yard, Burr Street, Wapping a Mr Abraham Constable was robbed of twelve shillings, and then the criminals repaired to an inn in the Minories to divide up the cash. Here Walter Nagle and Robert fall out. Walter accused Robert of hiding some gold obtained from Mr Constable, to which he replied, 'Damn your Blood, you thief and villain. I will blow your brains out.' Pulling out his pistol, Walter swore that he would blow out brains for brains. Francis, to prevent theft developing into murder, knocked the pistol out of Walter's hand and peace prevailed, and they divided out the cash.

Walter, now in a black mood, resolved with his accomplices to rob the first person he came across and went over to Tower Hill and, perhaps imprudently, attacked Mr Justice Willoughby who lived there. He levelled two blows with his stick on the judge, who fell to the floor. A companion of the judge, witnessing all this, rushed at Walter to prevent further damage. This hero called back to the tavern where he had been drinking with friends, for reinforcements, at which point Robert, Walter and Charles ran for it but they left Francis behind, whom Mr Justice Willoughby captured and with the help of the other witnesses had him locked up in the Tower prison. The next day he was before Mr Justice Dennet and, conscious of his guilt, gave evidence against the other three.

Richard and Walter, hearing that they had been betrayed, hid by enlisting on a privateer harbouring at Cowes on the Isle of Wight. No sooner were they on board than the crew mutinied. The two of them took to the shore in a longboat, but were arrested and locked up, Robert on *HMS Shrewsbury* and Walter on another man of war, from which he escaped by swimming ashore. The commanding officer of the *Shrewsbury* was taking no chances with Robert and had him chained in irons, in which condition he remained for six weeks. Finally an order came from the Admiralty to bring him to London and he was conveyed, handcuffed, by coach to Newgate gaol. At the Old Bailey the prosecution chose the robbery of Captain Pidgeon as the case to be heard. He was indicted with Walter, who was still at large. The Captain gave evidence to say that he was going home to Burr Street, and just as he approached the *King's Brewhouse* he saw four athletic-looking, well-dressed men with ruffs on the other side of the street talking and laughing. One of them came up to him and grabbed him by the shoulder and asked him to which ship he belonged. He replied that it was not their business, at which point one robber shoved him against some railings and put a pistol to the corner of his mouth. Another robber put another pistol to the other corner and told him that if he spoke, which was impossible, he would shoot him. Then they frisked him and took his money. A small girl came into the street and thinking that the Captain was her father, cried out. One of the pistols was redirected to the child. The robbery done, the Captain was set free. Robert was found guilty and sentenced to death. The robbery of Mr Justice Willoughby was to stay on the file. However, the sentence was commuted by the King to transportation for 14 years.

What became of Sarah? She came to a sticky end as well. In June 1746 she was arrested for forgery. She had tried the trick that Robert had taught her. With his help, she forged the will of a dead sailor, Nicholas Wollin and then went off to the Doctors Commons to prove it, and finally to the Navy office to claim the back wages of some 40 pounds. She was found guilty and condemned to death, but then she announced she was pregnant or, as the reports stated, 'pleaded her belly'. A jury of matrons was called to examine her, her condition confirmed, and her sentence commuted to deportation. She sailed on the *St George* in December 1747. Robert had gone earlier on the *Susannah*. Charles Cleaver would appear to be the only member of the gang to actually hang, although they all deserved to. There is no record of Walter Neagle ever being sentenced, so perhaps he was never apprehended.

Picture Credits and Notes on Sources

The basic outline for the history of the Quare family can be found on genealogical websites. Those used include *Ancestry.com, Thegenealogist.com, Findmypast.com* and *Myheritage.com*. Extra information is from the newspaper websites, *17th and 18th Century Burney Collection Newspapers* and *British Newspaper Archive*. The biography of Robert Rochead came from *Oldbaileyonline.com*.

Credit for pictures should go to Tudor Quare, Hyde Park Antiques, New York, Andy and Fiona Barnard, Cedric Martin, Country Life Archive, The Lavers and District Local History Society, the Worshipful Company of Clockmakers and Bonham's.

INDEX

Page numbers in bold type refer to illustrations